Food on a Stick Cookbook

Fair and Carnival

Food on a Stick Recipes

Louise Davidson

Copyrights

All rights reserved © Louise Davidson and The Cookbook Publisher. No part of this publication or the information in it may be quoted from or reproduced in any form by means such as printing, scanning, photocopying, or otherwise without prior written permission of the copyright holder.

Disclaimer and Terms of Use

Effort has been made to ensure that the information in this book is accurate and complete. However, the author and the publisher do not warrant the accuracy of the information, text, and graphics contained within the book due to the rapidly changing nature of science, research, known and unknown facts, and internet. The author and the publisher do not hold any responsibility for errors, omissions, or contrary interpretation of the subject matter herein. This book is presented solely for motivational and informational purposes only.

The recipes provided in this book are for informational purposes only and are not intended to provide dietary advice. A medical practitioner should be consulted before making any changes in diet. Additionally, recipe cooking times may require adjustment depending on age and quality of appliances. Readers are strongly urged to take all precautions to ensure ingredients are fully cooked in order to avoid the dangers of foodborne illnesses. The recipes and suggestions provided in this book are solely the opinion of the author. The author and publisher do not take any responsibility for any consequences that may result due to following the instructions provided in this book.

ISBN: 978-1548549688

Printed in the United States

Contents

Food Tastes Better on a Stick! 1
Savory Recipes 5
    The Classic Food on a Stick Corn Dogs 5
    Pork Chops on a Stick 7
    Steak Taco on a Stick 9
    Cheese Meatballs on a Stick 11
    Thai Chicken Skewers 13
    Tornado Potatoes 15
    Meatloaf on a Stick 17
    Pizza on a Stick 19
    Lasagna Rolls on a Stick 21
    Vegetarian Corn Dogs 23
    Caprese Kabob on a Stick 25
    Buffalo Wings on a Stick 26
    Mac and Cheese on a Stick 27
    Chicken and Zucchini Meat Balls on a Skewer 29
    Jerk Chicken Skewers 31
    Sushi Pops 33
    Spicy Salmon Lemon Kabobs 34
    Fish and Chips on a Stick 35
    Mini Burger on a Stick 37
    Caesar Salad on a Stick 39
    Spaghetti Meatballs on a Stick 41
    Lamb Skewer with Satay Sauce 43
    Ham and Cheese Ribbon on a Stick 45
    Deep Fried Ravioli on a Stick 46
    Bacon Wrapped Dates on a Stick 47
    Grilled Garlic Shrimp Skewers 48
    Tater Dog 49
    Sausages on a Stick 51
Sweet Recipes 53
    Rainbow Cake Push Pops 53
    Chocolate Banana on a Stick 55

Mango-Strawberry Ice Pops 56
Candy Bars on a Stick 57
Caramel and Chocolate Apple on a Stick 59
Cookie Pops 61
Fruity Fun Skewers 62
Donut on a Stick 63
Caramel Popcorn on a Stick 65
Cheesecake on a Stick 67
Cupcake on a Stick 69
Chocolate Kiwi Pops 71
Peach Pie on a Stick 72
Strawberry Shortcake on a Stick 73
S'mores Pops 74
Apple Fritters on a Stick 75
Banana Split Treats on a Stick 77
Fruity Ice Pops 78
Chocolate Bacon on a Stick 79
Pineapple Funnel Cake 81
Rainbow Lollipop 83
Hot Chocolate on a Stick 85
Pina Colada on a Stick 87
About the Author 89
  More Books by Louise Davidson 91
Appendix – Cooking Conversion Charts 95

Food Tastes Better on a Stick!

Food on a stick is believed to be among the earliest examples of human tool use. People have been cooking food on skewers for thousands of years. The first ever use of sticks were chopsticks. They were invented in ancient China, between 1122-1766 BC

Later with time, these chopsticks transformed into, wooden skewers, metal skewers, Popsicle sticks, lollipop sticks, and bamboo sticks. These items are now widely used for frying, grilling, and serving. Wooden skewers are sometimes small, often decorative, and can be used to garnish cocktails and other beverages.

Food on a stick has come a long way from cooking to serving especially when it comes to the fairground. It is one of the most attractive and charming parts of the fair. Food at the fair is one of the biggest attractions for millions of people. Food on a stick is automatically more fun to eat and enjoy, for every age group.

Corn dog is considered to be one of the classic foods which are served on sticks in America. Corn dogs were invented in 1940's, but they were popularized at Texas State Fair and the Minnesota State Fair, Ice pops and lollipops were already around.

When it comes to the creative food on sticks, how can we forget, the delicious and sticky confection treat, The Cotton Candy, which is the cornerstone of the American's fair and carnivals, for more than 100 years. Cotton candy isn't a modern invention. It was first introduced in 1897 by William Morrison and John C. Warton at the St. Louis World's Fair as "Fairy Floss".Later the name was changed to the Cotton Candy.

There are tons of food that can be skewered, sticks are not only reserved for only corn dogs, popsicles, lollipops, and candy apples. Around one-third of the world population uses sticks for eating.

"National Something on a Stick Day" is celebrated on March 28 which uses creative talents from worldwide. This holiday celebrates food on a stick like popsicles, kabobs, corndogs, and cake, etc...

Cotton candy was originally called "fairy floss." This is because the cotton candy machine turns the sugar into a very light stringy substance that is then collected on the stick. Fairy floss became known as cotton candy in 1920. National Cotton Candy Day is celebrated on November 7 each year.

Ice pops were invented by an 11-year-old boy named Frank Epperson in 1905 when he accidentally left a cup of homemade soda in the freezer overnight. He called it the Epsicle which was later changed to Popsicles. The first customers to buy ice pops were Epperson's classmates!

The most popular flavors of ice pops are Cherry and Strawberry. Over two billions of ice pops are sold each year.

The corn dog was first introduced in 1929 by a German immigrant in Texas. The Texas State fair sells the most corn dogs of all fairs in America with 630,000 corn dogs sold per season.

The Wisconsin state fair offers some crazy food like "Deep-Fried Butter on sticks."

More than 80 delicious and creative foods are sold on a stick at State Fairs.

George Smith was the first to invent the modern style lollipop, which were derived from the term "lolly" (tongue) and "pop" (slap) and it was first trademarked in 1931.

If you think these stick treats are too hard to make, something that can only be found in state fairs, and can't be replicated at home, then think again. The truth is, they're as easy as pie to make in the comfort of your home.

This book offer a collection of 50 typical fair-style food on a stick recipes with assertive flavors that can be easily achieved at home.

Recipes include main courses and traditional meals where you'll get the best of Buffalo wings to the meatloaf on a stick, Sushi pops to the Pork chops on a stick.

And for the sweet tooth, you'll get the most popular stick delicacies, from the S'more pops to strawberry shortcake on a stick, hot chocolate to cheesecake on a stick, and many more. Try these homemade versions of classic food recipes on a stick and explore the fun of fairs and carnival at your home.

Savory Recipes

The Classic Food on a Stick Corn Dogs

Serves 15

Ingredients

15 hot dogs

1 cup all-purpose flour

1 cup yellow cornmeal

1 egg, beaten

1 tablespoon granulated sugar

3 tablespoons honey

1 teaspoon baking powder

½ cup of buttermilk

1 tablespoon vegetable oil

½ teaspoon salt

Vegetable oil for frying

15 wooden skewers

Directions

1. In an electric skillet or deep-fryer, heat oil to 350° F.
2. In a large mixing bowl add all the dry ingredients.
3. In a separate bowl beat egg, honey, buttermilk, and oil.
4. Now add the liquid ingredients into the dry ingredients and stir until well combined.

5. Let it set for 15 minutes.
6. Wipe the hot dogs with paper towels until dry. Insert the sticks into hot dogs vertically.
7. Pour the batter into a drinking glass and dunk each hot dog into batter, making sure to coat it evenly.
8. Now immediately place the hot dogs into the hot oil, fry until golden brown.
9. Remove from the oil and place them on paper towels to drain excess oil.
10. Follow the same procedure until all of them are done.

Pork Chops on a Stick

Serves 6

Ingredients

6 boneless Pork chops, 1 1/2 inches thick

3 tablespoons soy sauce

Juice from 1 lemon

Salt and pepper to taste

6 thick wooden skewers or bamboo chopsticks

<u>Rub</u>

¼ teaspoon garlic, crushed

¼ teaspoon freshly ground ginger

¼ teaspoon onion salt

¼ teaspoon dry mustard

¼ teaspoon ground cumin

1 tablespoon granulated white sugar

Directions

1. Add the chops to a re-sealable plastic bag and add soy sauce and lemon juice.
2. To make the rub, combine all the ingredients in a small bowl. Add to the bag and gently rub the spices on the chops.
3. Refrigerate the chops in rub for at least 1 hour.
4. When ready to cook, preheat the grill pan on medium heat.
5. Insert the skewers into the short side of each chop.

6. Place the chops on a grill pan.
7. Cover and grill for 30 to 35 minutes or until chops are slightly pink in the center and juices run clear. Let the chops rest for 10 minutes before serving.

Steak Taco on a Stick

Serves 30

Ingredients

2 pounds sirloin steaks, cut into 1 inch cubes

For marinade:

1 teaspoon garlic powder

1 teaspoon ground ginger

1 teaspoon onion powder

½ cup soy sauce

2 tablespoons molasses or honey

¼ cup olive oil

¼ cup water

2 teaspoons mustard powder

⅓ cup lemon juice

½ teaspoon salt

For assembling:

1 avocado, cut into ½ inch chunks

2 ears corn, cut into 1 inch slices

1 small red onion

2 flour tortillas cut into triangles

Salsa and lime wedges, for serving

30 wooden skewers or thick bamboo sticks, soaked 30 minutes in water before using

Directions

1. To prepare the marinade, whisk together all the marinade ingredients in a medium bowl.
2. Add in meat pieces and toss until evenly coated.
3. Refrigerate for at least 6-8 hours or for overnight for intense flavor.
4. Preheat the grill to high.
5. Thread beef then avocado, corn, onions, and tortilla triangles onto skewer.
6. Grill for 8 to 10 minutes, turning halfway through, and brushing remaining marinade onto each skewer.
7. Serve with salsa and lime wedges.

Cheese Meatballs on a Stick

Serves 12

Ingredients

1 tube refrigerated breadstick dough

1 ½ cups shredded mozzarella cheese

Marinara sauce, for serving

12 skewers

<u>Meatballs</u>

1 pound lean ground beef

½ pound lean ground pork

¼ cup shredded Parmesan cheese

¼ cup onion, finely chopped

¼ cup fresh parsley, chopped

2 eggs

⅓ cup bread crumbs

1 teaspoon Dijon mustard

¼ teaspoon thyme

½ teaspoon crushed red pepper

¼ teaspoon freshly ground black pepper

2 teaspoons garlic, minced

½ teaspoon salt

Directions

1. Preheat the oven to 375° F. Line 2 baking sheets with parchment paper.
2. In a medium bowl, combine all of the meat ingredients.
3. Gently mix all the meatball ingredients with your hand until combined evenly.
4. Shape the meat mixture into small size balls, about 1 – 1 1/2-inch in diameter.
5. Unroll the breadstick dough and cut into 12 strips.
6. Thread one end of breadstick on skewer, add one meat ball then thread the dough again over meatball.
7. Repeat this threading sequence with the breadstick and 2 meatballs, ending the threading with the dough strip.
8. Transfer the skewers onto baking sheet and bake for 20 to 22 minutes, or until meatballs are cooked through and breadsticks are nice golden brown.
9. Once finished, sprinkle the meatballs with grated mozzarella cheese and broil for additional 3 minutes or until cheese has melted.
10. Serve warm with marinara sauce.

Thai Chicken Skewers

Serves 12

Ingredients

3 pounds boneless chicken

¼ cup soy sauce

3 tablespoons vinegar

1 tablespoon red chili powder

2 teaspoons lemon zest

5 tablespoons coconut cream

3 tablespoons dark brown sugar

3 garlic cloves

1 teaspoon ground ginger

2 tablespoons heavy cream

2 tablespoons olive oil

1 tablespoon curry powder

¼ teaspoon ground cardamom

½ teaspoon salt

12 wooden skewers

Directions
1. In a blender mix together all the ingredients except the chicken.
2. In a large bowl mix the marinade with chicken until evenly coated.
3. Cover the bowl with plastic wrap and refrigerate for 5-6 hours or overnight for a flavorful taste.
4. Thread the marinated chicken onto wooden skewers.
5. Grease the grill with some olive oil and grill the chicken for 15-20 minutes until chicken is cooked through. Rotate skewers halfway through to cook evenly on both sides.
6. Serve hot with your favorite sauce and lime wedges.

Tornado Potatoes

Serves 6

Ingredients

6 large potatoes

2 tablespoons cornstarch

½ teaspoon oregano

½ teaspoon paprika

½ teaspoon black pepper

¼ teaspoon thyme

¼ teaspoon chili powder

Chili sauce to taste

6 wooden skewers

Oil for frying

Directions

1. Wash potatoes thoroughly. Cut a small slice from the top of the potatoes.
2. Insert the skewer in the middle of the cut all the way through the potato. With a sharp knife, cut the potatoes in a spiral, down to the skewer following the same direction.
3. Then separate each spiral carefully spreading it along the skewer.
4. Sprinkle some cornstarch over the potatoes and set aside until ready to fry.
5. In a small bowl mix together all the spices except the chili sauce.

6. Heat the oil 350°F and fry them until crisp and golden brown.
7. When finished frying, drain the potatoes on a paper towel.
8. Sprinkle with some mixed spices and chili sauce and enjoy!

Meatloaf on a Stick

Serves 8

Ingredients

1 pound lean ground meat (Beef, Turkey, or Chicken)

10 mozzarella sticks, ½ inch thick

1 cup spaghetti sauce

½ cup green diced peppers (optional)

1 large egg, lightly beaten

1 cup seasoned bread crumbs

2 garlic cloves, minced

1 ½ teaspoons dried rosemary

1 tablespoon Worcestershire sauce

1 teaspoon black pepper

Salt to taste

8 Popsicle sticks

Directions

1. Preheat the oven to 400° F.
2. Mix crumbled meat, spaghetti sauce, diced peppers, bread crumbs, egg, garlic, rosemary, Worcestershire sauce, black pepper, and salt in a large bowl. Mix until well combined.
3. Insert the Popsicle sticks into the mozzarella stick, and evenly coat the meat mixture around the cheese stick. Lightly pat the meat to make it stick.

4. Place the sticks on a greased cookie sheet and bake for 1 1/2 hours or until meat is cooked through.
5. Serve with your favorite sauce.

Pizza on a Stick

Serves 12

Ingredients

For the pizza dough:
2 ½ cups bread flour

1 package or 25 ounces active dry yeast

1 cup warm milk or water

2 tablespoons of olive oil

1 tablespoon sugar

1 teaspoon salt

1 teaspoon dry milk powder

For filling:
1 cup pepperoni or sausages, sliced

1 cup pizza sauce

½ cup cherry tomatoes

2 cups grated mozzarella cheese

1 cup whole fresh mushrooms

1 large green pepper, sliced

1 medium sized onion, sliced

Salt and black pepper to taste

12 Popsicle sticks

Directions

For pizza dough:
1. In a mixing bowl add yeast, sugar, and water. Let stand for 15 minutes.
2. Now stir in rest of the dough ingredients. Beat until smooth. Let stand for 5-7 minutes.
3. Place the dough onto a lightly floured surface. Knead for 3 minutes.
4. Let stand for 15-20 minutes covered.

Assembling:
1. Preheat oven to 400° F.
2. Roll the pizza dough on lightly floured surface, into a thick rectangle.
3. Place the pizza sauce, vegetables, and pepperoni on top.
4. Now add cheese, salt, and pepper.
5. Roll the dough into a log.
6. Cut small ¼ thick bite size buns.
7. Insert the sticks into the buns vertically to keep the roll from becoming unraveled.
8. Place it on a baking sheet, cover with plastic wrap and let stand for 15-20 minutes. Remove the plastic wrap before placing in the oven.
9. Now bake for 15-20 minutes or until nice golden brown. Serve and enjoy!

Lasagna Rolls on a Stick

Serves 20

Ingredients

1 package lasagna noodles

1 pound lean ground beef

3 cloves garlic

10 ounces Baby spinach

1 large onion, diced

1 cup pasta sauce

1 can mushroom pieces

15 ounces ricotta cheese

1 cup shredded mozzarella cheese

¼ cup parmesan cheese

2 tablespoons olive oil

¼ teaspoon black pepper

½ teaspoon salt

20 wooden skewers

Directions

1. Preheat oven to 350°F. Line the baking tray with parchment paper.
2. Cook noodles according to the package directions.
3. In a medium size pan, heat oil and fry onion. Add garlic and beef stirring occasionally.

4. Stir in pasta sauce and mushrooms and cook for additional 10 minutes.
5. Remove from heat and set aside.
6. In a large mixing bowl, mix spinach, ricotta cheese, mozzarella cheese, parmesan, salt, and pepper.
7. Pat noodles dry with a paper towel and place them on baking sheet.
8. Cut each noodle in half and place a teaspoon of beef mixture with 2 tablespoons of cheese mixture onto noodle and start rolling.
9. Insert a skewer into each roll to keep from unraveling. Top each roll with a teaspoon of pasta sauce and some parmesan cheese.
10. Place each skewer onto tray. Cover the tray with foil and bake for 12 to 15 minutes until cheese is melted.
11. Serve warm.

Vegetarian Corn Dogs

Serves 12

Ingredients

6 tofu hot dogs or vegetarian hot dogs

½ cup all-purpose flour

½ cup yellow cornmeal

1 teaspoon dry mustard

1 egg substitute or ¼ cup of unsweetened applesauce

1 tablespoon sugar

1 teaspoon baking powder

½ cup of soymilk

1 tablespoon vegetable shortening

12 skewers or thick bamboo sticks

Directions

1. In deep fryer, heat oil at 375° F.
2. Combine the flour, cornmeal, sugar, baking powder, dry mustard, and salt and mix well.
3. In a separate bowl, mix together soymilk, egg substitute or applesauce, and shortening.
4. Add the wet ingredients to the dry ingredients, mix until well combined.
5. Pour the mixture into a long container or a glass.
6. Insert the skewer into hot dogs.

7. Dip the hot dogs into the batter and fry until nice golden brown.

8. Drain the excess oil on paper towel and serve.

Caprese Kabob on a Stick

Serves 20

Ingredients

20 fresh basil leaves

20 mini mozzarella, 1 inch cubes

20 cherry tomatoes

1 cup Balsamic vinegar

Black pepper to taste

Salt to taste

20 skewers

Directions

1. Thread the cherry tomatoes, basil leaves, and mozzarella cubes onto skewers. Following the same sequence until the skewer is covered.
2. Sprinkle with some salt and pepper.
3. Place the balsamic vinegar in a small pot and bring it to simmer on low heat for 10 minutes or until it thickens.
4. Remove from heat, let cool, and then drizzle it over the top of the kabobs.

Buffalo Wings on a Stick

Serves 13

Ingredients

16 chicken wings

¾ cup Buffalo wings sauce

2 tablespoons melted butter

8 wooden skewers

Directions

1. Preheat oven to 400° F.
2. Mix together buffalo wing sauce and butter.
3. Toss the wings in the sauce and thread 2 wings onto each skewer.
4. Place the wing skewer on baking sheet lined with parchment paper.
5. Bake for 30 to 40 minutes until nicely golden brown, taking care of turning over halfway through.

Mac and Cheese on a Stick

Serves 10

Ingredients

1 pound elbow macaroni

1 pound cheddar cheese

3 tablespoons all-purpose flour

2 cups milk

2 tablespoons butter

1 tablespoon thick heavy cream

Salt and pepper to taste

Oil for frying

10 wooden skewers

For the dredge:
3 cups bread crumbs

2 cups all-purpose flour

3 eggs

½ teaspoon salt

Directions

1. Cook the macaroni according to the package instructions.
2. Rinse with cold water. Drain and mix 1 teaspoon of oil and let stand for 10 minutes.

For sauce:
1. In a medium size saucepan melt the butter, add flour, and cook for 1-2 minutes whisking continuously.

2. Slowly add in milk, stirring continuously so there are no lumps.
3. Remove from heat and add in cream, cheese, salt, and black pepper.
4. Now fold the macaroni into the sauce. Make sure to mix well.
5. Refrigerate for 3-4 hours or until set and firm enough to handle with hands.
6. Make small meatball-sized balls and place them onto a baking sheet.
7. Take two separate bowls, one for the bread crumbs and second for flour.
8. Whisk together egg, salt, and pepper in a third bowl.
9. Coat the mac and cheese balls in the flour.
10. Dip them into egg mixture and then into bread crumbs.
11. Place them onto a baking sheet and freeze for another hour.
12. Heat the oil in a deep fryer to 400° F.
13. Fry the mac and cheese balls for 5 minutes or until they are nice golden brown.
14. Place 2 balls on each skewer and serve hot.

Chicken and Zucchini Meat Balls on a Skewer

Serves 24

Ingredients

1 cup zucchini, fine shredded

1 pound ground chicken

2 green onions, sliced

4 tablespoons cilantro, finely chopped

2 cloves garlic

1 tablespoon honey

½ teaspoon black pepper

1 teaspoon salt

Olive oil, for cooking

24 wooden skewers or thick bamboo sticks

Salsa, guacamole, or any other favorite dip for serving

Directions

1. Squeeze out the liquid of shredded zucchini with your hands.
2. In a large mixing bowl mix together zucchini, chicken, green onions, cilantro, garlic, honey, pepper and salt.
3. Warm the olive oil in a large skillet over medium heat.
4. Using your hands or a small scoop make 1-inch size meatballs.

5. Cook for about 10-15 minutes or until balls are golden brown on every sides and cooked through. Cook in batches and make sure not to overcrowd the skillet.

6. Insert the skewer into balls and serve with salsa, guacamole, or your favorite dip.

Jerk Chicken Skewers

Serves 12

Ingredients

2 pounds chicken breast, diced into ½ inch thick cubes

1 finely chopped onion

4 roughly chopped scallions

1 teaspoon garlic, crushed

1 teaspoon ginger, finely chopped

2 teaspoons fresh thyme leaves

½ teaspoon ground nutmeg

½ teaspoon ground cinnamon

1 teaspoon ground black pepper

3 tablespoons soy sauce

1 tablespoon cooking oil

2 tablespoons granulated sugar

1 tablespoon fresh lime juice

1 tablespoon apple cider vinegar

1 teaspoon salt

12 wooden skewers

For sauce:
1 pound cucumber, peeled and roughly chopped

½ cup sour cream

¾ cup mayonnaise

⅛ cup apple cider vinegar

1 tablespoon Dijon mustard

1 tablespoon garlic, chopped

1 teaspoon salt

Directions
1. In a small mixing bowl mix together onion, scallion, ginger, garlic, thyme, all spices, soy sauce, sugar, oil, lemon juice, vinegar, salt, and pepper. These ingredients can also be combined in a food processor.
2. Place this mixture in a Ziploc bag and add the chicken cubes. Seal tightly.
3. Refrigerate and let marinate for 1 to 2 hours.
4. In the meantime, prepare the dipping sauce. Mix all the ingredients in a blender and puree. Set aside.
5. Thread the marinated chicken cubes onto the skewers and grill for 5 to 6 minutes or until the meat is firm and the juices run clear.
6. Serve with dipping sauce.

Sushi Pops

Serves 8

Ingredients

1 Nori sheet

⅔ cup sushi rice, cooked

6 sticks surimi or shrimp

1 whole avocado

½ cup sriracha hot sauce

½ teaspoon sea salt

8 Popsicle sticks

Directions

1. Cover the bamboo mat or sushi mat with plastic wrap.
2. Place nori sheet and cut into half. Place the shiny side facing down.
3. Now gently spread the sushi rice and pat it in an even layer using the back of spoon.
4. Spoon the sriracha sauce, followed by the surimi, sliced avocado, and salt.
5. Carefully roll it inside out.
6. Cut into 8 small pieces.
7. Insert sticks and serve.

Spicy Salmon Lemon Kabobs

Serves 12

Ingredients

1 1/2 pounds skinless salmon fillet, cut into 1 inch pieces

2 tablespoons oregano

1 teaspoon ground cumin

¼ teaspoon red chili flakes

2 teaspoons sesame seed

2 tablespoons olive oil

3 lemons, thinly sliced

1 teaspoon freshly ground black pepper

1 teaspoon salt

Chopped cilantro, for garnishing

¼ cup olive oil, for brushing

12 bamboo skewers

Directions

1. Heat grill to high.
2. Mix all the ingredients except cilantro and oil for brushing together with salmon, set aside.
3. Alternately thread salmon and lemon slices onto skewers.
4. Brush with oil and grill for 6 to 8 minutes, turning occasionally until the salmon is opaque and cooked through.
5. Garnish with chopped cilantro and serve.

Fish and Chips on a Stick

Serves 8

Ingredients

1 pound white fish fillets such as tilapia or cod

4 large potatoes

½ cup all-purpose flour

¼ cup cornstarch

½ teaspoon baking soda

1 tablespoon vinegar

⅔ cup ice cold water

½ teaspoon salt

Oil for frying

Tartar Sauce for serving

8 wooden skewers

Directions

1. Cut the fish fillets into 1½-inch cubes.
2. In a shallow dish, mix flour, cornstarch, baking soda, and salt.
3. Add in vinegar and ice cold water. Mix until smooth and lump free. Refrigerate for 15 minutes.
4. Peel and shred the potatoes. Add potatoes in a large bowl filled with cold water, to dissolve starch stir the potatoes until water is cloudy. Drain and squeeze out the excess water.
5. Heat the oil at 300° F.

6. Spread the shredded potatoes on a baking sheet, and keep the refrigerated batter next to it.

7. Thread the fish onto skewer. Dunk the fish skewers into the batter, make sure to coat it evenly. Let excess batter drip off batter into the bowl. Place the fish skewers onto the shredded potatoes, press gently and roll to help the potatoes adhere to each side of fish.

8. Fry each fish fillet until crispy and golden brown. Drain the excess oil on paper towel and serve with tartar sauce.

Mini Burger on a Stick

Serves 10

Ingredients

For burger patties:
1 pound lean ground beef

3 tablespoons onions finely chopped

4 tablespoons bread crumbs

2 tablespoons milk

2 tablespoons Worcestershire sauce

1 tablespoon soy sauce

1 teaspoon black pepper

½ teaspoon salt

2 tablespoons olive oil

For assembling:
10-12 flat bread pieces

5-6 lettuce leaves

6 slices American cheese

6 grape tomatoes, halved

Mayonnaise

BBQ Sauce

10 Skewers

Directions

1. Cut small round pieces of flat bread using the round cutter. Set aside.

2. Mix together ground beef, onion, bread crumbs, milk, Worcestershire sauce, soy sauce, black pepper, and salt.

3. Make small meatballs and flatten with the palm of your hand, according to the size of the bread cut outs.

4. In a nonstick skillet pan, warm the olive oil over medium heat. Fry the burger patties until nice golden brown.

Assembling:

1. Now assemble the burger bites. Start with the bread cut outs. Place mayonnaise, lettuce, and a burger on the bread. Add a dollop of BBQ sauce and cheese slice, covered it with another piece of bread. Insert the skewer into the burgers and top it off with half grape tomato.

Caesar Salad on a Stick

Serves 12

Ingredients

Caesar salad dressing:
6 anchovy fillets, mashed

2 small garlic cloves, finely chopped

2 egg yolks

2 tablespoons olive oil

½ teaspoon Dijon mustard

½ cup vegetable oil

3 tablespoons grated parmesan

1 teaspoon lemon juice

½ teaspoon freshly ground black pepper

Salt to taste

Other ingredients
1 head romaine lettuce chopped

12 cherry tomatoes

10 ounces shaved parmesan cheese

1 package croutons

½ teaspoon black pepper

Salt to taste

12 skewers

Directions

1. To make the dressing, whisk egg yolk, mustard, and lemon juice. Add anchovy fillets, garlic, olive oil, and salt. Pour the olive oil slowly, few drops at a time while whisking constantly. Once the dressing has started to thicken, whisk in the 3 tablespoons of parmesan. Season with some salt and pepper.
2. Chop the lettuce into small ½-inch chunks.
3. Toss the lettuce and tomatoes in the Caesar dressing.
4. Thread lettuce, tomato, and then crouton onto skewer.
5. Place the skewers onto a baking sheet lined with waxed paper. Sprinkle with some parmesan cheese, salt, and pepper. Place in the refrigerator until ready to serve.

Spaghetti Meatballs on a Stick

Serves 15

Ingredients

1 package spaghetti

1 pound lean ground beef

1 onion, finely diced

1 teaspoon minced garlic

1 large egg

¼ cup fresh basil, chopped

1 tablespoon olive oil

1 cup spaghetti sauce

1 cup grated parmesan cheese

¼ teaspoon black pepper

Salt to taste

15 wooden skewers

Directions

1. Cook spaghetti according to the package instructions. Drain and place in a shallow bowl.
2. In a large mixing bowl add beef, egg, cheese, onion, oil, garlic, basil, salt, and black pepper.
3. Roll into 1-inch balls.
4. In a non-stick frying pan heat olive oil and cook meat balls for 5 minutes.

5. Pour the spaghetti sauce and cook for additional 5 to 10 minutes or until meatball is cooked through. Remove from heat.

6. Twirl 6 to 8 spaghetti strands around skewer, insert into meatball.

7. Serve warm.

Lamb Skewer with Satay Sauce

Serves 12

Ingredients

1 pound lamb meat

½ teaspoon black pepper

Salt to taste

12 wooden skewer or bamboo sticks, soaked in cold water for 30 minutes before using

<u>For the sauce</u>
2 tablespoons peanut oil

1 onion, finely diced

4 cloves garlic, minced

2 tablespoons soy sauce

⅓ cup sweet chili sauce

1 tablespoon hoisin sauce

1 tablespoon fish sauce

1 tablespoon sugar

1 cup crunchy peanut butter

1 ¼ cups coconut milk

2 tablespoons olive oil

1 teaspoon black pepper

Salt to taste

Directions

1. Cut lamb meat into 1-inch cubes. Thread closely onto skewers. Sprinkle with some salt and black pepper.
2. Place on a baking sheet covered with plastic wrap and refrigerate for 30 minutes.
3. To make the sauce, heat peanut oil in a frying pan. Over medium heat Add onion and garlic. Cook for 2 to 3 minutes until light golden brown. Add all the remaining ingredients, stirring occasionally for 10 minutes. If the consistency is too thick add water to make it thinner. Remove from heat and set aside.
4. Preheat an outdoor barbecue grill or a grilling pan over medium heat. Grease the pan or grill with olive oil.
5. Transfer the lamb skewers onto the grilling pan, and cook for 3 to 5 minutes until the lamb is cooked through. Turn over halfway through.
6. Serve with satay sauce.

Ham and Cheese Ribbon on a Stick

Serves 8

Ingredients

8 slices smoked ham

10 ounces cheddar cheese

10 ounces Monterey jack cheese

20 cherry tomatoes

10 baby dill pickles, ½ inch slice

2 tablespoons Dijon mustard

8 wooden skewers

Directions

1. Cut the cheeses into 3/4 inch cube.
2. Thread one end of ham strip into skewer, then one cheese cube, bring the strip of ham over cheese.
3. Now add one cherry tomato and bring the ham strip over tomato and onto skewer.
4. Add one piece of pickle and repeat the same wrapping technique over each ingredient and skewer.
5. Serve with Dijon mustard.

Deep Fried Ravioli on a Stick

Serves 6

Ingredients

3-4 cups vegetable oil for deep frying

18 store-bought frozen raviolis

1 cup buttermilk or 2 eggs beaten

½ cups bread crumbs

¼ cup grated parmesan

Vegetable oil for frying

6 wooden sticks

Directions

1. Preheat vegetable oil in a large, heavy pot over medium-high heat.
2. Place the breadcrumbs and buttermilk in separate shallow dishes.
3. Working in batches, dip the ravioli in butter milk then in bread crumbs until evenly coated.
4. Thread 3 to 4 ravioli onto each skewer.
5. Fry the ravioli in hot oil, turning occasionally until golden brown.
6. Drain on paper towels.
7. Sprinkle the fried ravioli with some parmesan and serve.

Bacon Wrapped Dates on a Stick

Serves 20

Ingredients

1 pound thinly sliced bacon

16 large Medjool dates

4 ounces goat cheese

4 ounces almonds

20 wooden skewers

Directions

1. Preheat the oven to 400° Fahrenheit.
2. Remove the pit by slitting the dates lengthwise on one side to create an opening.
3. Using a small spoon, stuff a small amount of goat cheese into the palm of your hand and place one almond in the middle of cheese, make a small round ball.
4. Place the cheese ball inside the date.
5. Stuff each date with the cheese ball, then wrap in bacon slice, and secure with a toothpick.
6. Place the dates on a baking sheet and bake for 10 minutes until bacon is golden brown and crisp.

Grilled Garlic Shrimp Skewers

Serves 12

Ingredients

1 ½ pounds large shrimp, peeled and deveined

8 tablespoons unsalted butter

2 teaspoons garlic minced

1 tablespoon Cajun spice

1 tablespoon lemon juice

Freshly ground black pepper, to taste

¼ teaspoon salt

5 medium size lemon wedges

12 medium-length wooden skewers soaked in cold water for 30 minutes before using

Directions

1. Preheat grill medium to high heat at 400° F.
2. In a small sauce pan combine all the ingredients except shrimp and lemon wedges. Bring to a simmer on low heat.
3. Transfer the marinade into a small bowl.
4. Thread 4 shrimps and 1 or 2 lemon wedges onto skewers. Place the shrimp skewers onto a baking sheet and brush each side with marinade and refrigerate for 5 minutes until butter firms up.
5. Grill the shrimp skewers for 2-3 minutes or until cooked through. Don't overcook or they will be tough, rubbery, and dry.
6. Brush with the remaining sauce and serve.

Tater Dog

Serves 8

Ingredients

2 Russet potatoes

8 hot dogs

½ cup flour

1 tablespoon paprika

1 tablespoon onion powder

1 tablespoon garlic powder

1 egg

1 teaspoon freshly ground black pepper

½ teaspoon salt

Oil for frying

8 wooden chopsticks

Directions

1. Heat oil in deep fryer to 350F
2. In a mixing bowl, add flour, paprika, onion powder, garlic powder, black pepper, and salt.
3. Add one egg and mix again until it forms a smooth creamy batter.
4. Finely shred the potatoes and soak in cold water for 15 minutes to remove the excess starch.
5. Drain the potatoes on paper towel, squeezing out the remaining moisture.

6. Add the shredded potatoes with the egg batter, mix until well combined.
7. Now thread the hot dogs and dip in the egg batter.
8. Using your hands, press the potato mixture evenly around each hot dog and then fry until golden brown, about 5-7 minutes each.

Sausages on a Stick

Serves 12

Ingredients

11 ounces refrigerated breadsticks dough or pizza dough

12 hot dogs

Ketchup or mustard for dipping

12 wooden skewers

Nonstick cooking spray

Directions

1. Preheat oven to 350° F.
2. Roll the dough out, about 1 inch thickness, then cut it into 10 to 12, 10 inch long strips.
3. Insert the skewer into each hot dog and wrap the dough strip in a spiral, from the top of the hot dog to the end.
4. Place the hot dogs on a baking sheet greased with cooking spray.
5. Bake for 10 to 12 minutes until nicely puffed and golden brown.
6. Serve with your favorite dip.

Sweet Recipes

Rainbow Cake Push Pops

Serves 6

Ingredients

<u>Cake batter</u>
1 ½ cups self-rising flour

¾ cup unsalted butter

1 cup sugar

½ cup milk

2 large eggs, beaten

1 teaspoon pure vanilla extract

5 paste food colors of your choice (yellow, red, purple, blue or green)

<u>For butter cream</u>
2 cups confectioners' sugar9

½ cup unsalted butter

1 tablespoon milk

½ teaspoon pure vanilla extract

1 cup raspberry jam

Rainbow sprinkles to decorate

Cake push up containers

Directions

1. Preheat oven to 400°F. Line cupcake pan(s) with paper liners.

2. In a large mixing bowl, beat sugar and butter for 3 minutes. Add eggs and beat well. Add the flour, milk, and vanilla together, beat until well combined.

3. Separate the batter into 5 equal parts. Mix in a distinct color for each. Place 2 teaspoons of colored batter into each cupcake liner. You will need to 6 cupcake liners per color. Work in batches, if required. Bake for 15-20 minutes or until cooked through. Remove from the oven and transfer to a wire rack to cool down.

4. Meanwhile for the frosting, cream the butter and sugar together. Beat in vanilla extract. Add the milk and beat again until it forms a smooth and creamy frosting.

5. To assemble, cut the cakes using the push pop mold. Spread a spoonful of jam on one side of the each circle. Drop 1 circle into the push-up pop container. Top each circle with a spoonful of frosting, then add another layer of sponge cake jam and butter cream, until it forms a rainbow stack.

6. Finish the pops with a dollop of frosting and sprinkles, refrigerate for about 30 minutes.

7. Serve and Enjoy.

Chocolate Banana on a Stick

Serves 15

Ingredients

5 medium sized bananas

1 cup dark chocolate chips, melted

3 teaspoons butter

½ cup chopped peanuts

½ cup shredded coconut

½ cup rainbow sprinkles

15 wooden skewers

Directions

1. Cut bananas into 1 inch chunks.
2. Thread banana chunks onto the skewer and place them on a baking sheet.
3. Freeze for an hour.
4. In a small bowl melt chocolate chips and butter together.
5. Dip the banana skewers in melted chocolate mixture and place them back on to the baking sheet.
6. Top with any of your favorite topping, peanuts, shredded coconut, or rainbow sprinkles.
7. Freeze again for another ½ an hour until chocolate sets.

Mango-Strawberry Ice Pops

Serves 5

Ingredients

2 cups coconut milk

2 cups frozen mango, chunks

1 tablespoon heavy cream

1 cup frozen strawberries, sliced

3 tablespoons honey

1 tablespoon vanilla extract

Directions

1. Puree coconut milk, cream, mango, honey, and vanilla in a blender until thoroughly blended.
2. Pour the small amount of mango puree into push up pop mold, add sliced strawberry, and pour the puree again.
3. Freeze until solid and serve.

Candy Bars on a Stick

Serves 30

Ingredients

1 ½ cups all-purpose flour

¼ cup granulated sugar

2 teaspoons baking powder

⅛ teaspoon salt

¼ teaspoon ground cinnamon

1 large egg

¼ cup milk

1 ½ cups water

1 teaspoon vanilla extract

Mini candy bars (Snickers, Mars, Twix, or Milky Way)

1 cup melted dark chocolate

Oil for deep-fat frying

30 wooden skewers

Directions

1. In a large mixing bowl, whisk together flour, baking powder, sugar, salt, and cinnamon.
2. In another separate bowl add egg, water, milk, and vanilla extract.
3. Add the wet ingredients to the dry ingredients and mix until it's smooth and creamy.
4. In a deep fryer, heat oil to 350°F.

5. Insert the skewers into each candy bar.
6. Dip the mini candy bars into the batter and fry until light golden brown.
7. Insert a wooden skewer into each candy bar.
8. Drain the excess oil on paper towel.
9. Drizzle with some melted chocolate.

Caramel and Chocolate Apple on a Stick

Serves 12

Ingredients

2 cups sugar

½ cup water

¼ cup corn syrup

½ cup heavy cream

3 tablespoons butter

1 teaspoon vanilla extract

⅛ teaspoon salt

12 medium sized apples, washed and dried

1 cup dark chocolate, melted

1 cup white chocolate, melted

1 cup peanuts, chopped

12 Popsicle sticks

Directions

1. In a small saucepan, mix together sugar, corn syrup, and water. Bring to boil on medium heat.
2. Cook until the sugar is completely dissolved and candy thermometer reads 320°F.
3. Remove from the heat and add in cream, butter, vanilla extract, and salt.

4. Return to low heat, stirring continuously until smooth and creamy.
5. Let it set until the caramel is thick enough to coat the apples.
6. Insert the Popsicle sticks into the apples and dip them in the caramel.
7. Place the apples on a parchment-lined tray and let stand at room temperature until completely set.
8. Once the apples are set, drizzle with white and dark chocolate.
9. Sprinkle with some chopped peanuts.
10. Let cool and serve.

Cookie Pops

Serves 12

Ingredients

1 package sugar cookie dough

1 cup melted white chocolate

Assorted candy melts, for drizzling

1 cup rainbow sprinkles (for decoration, optional)

Assorted candies (for decoration)

10 yards curling ribbon (optional)

12 Popsicle sticks or wooden skewers

Directions

1. Preheat oven to 350° F and line a cookie sheet with parchment paper.
2. Roll the cookie dough on a clean surface and cut out heart shaped cookies using a 1 inch heart-cookie cutter.
3. Insert Popsicle sticks into each cookie and place it on the parchment paper.
4. Refrigerate for 15 minutes.
5. Take the cookies out and bake for 12 to 16 minutes or until light golden brown.
6. Cool completely, about 10 minutes.
7. Decorate with melted white chocolate, candies, and sprinkles.
8. Make a bow out of ribbon and stick next to cookie.

Fruity Fun Skewers

Serves 20

Ingredients

10 large strawberries

½ cup cantaloupe

3 bananas

1 cup grapes

1 cup pineapple

1 cup kiwi sliced

2 apples

1 cup whipping cream

20 skewers

Directions

1. Cut all the fruits into 1 to ½ inch of thick chunks.
2. Insert the skewer first into strawberry, then cantaloupe, then banana, then 2 grapes, then pineapple, then kiwi and apple. Serve with cream and enjoy.

Donut on a Stick

Serves 12

Ingredients

1 cup all-purpose flour

¼ cup granulated sugar

½ cup buttermilk

2 tablespoons butter

1 large egg

1 teaspoon baking powder

1 teaspoon vanilla extract

¼ teaspoon of salt

12 lollipop sticks or skewers

<u>For cinnamon donuts:</u>
½ cup confectioner's sugar

1 tablespoon cinnamon

Melted chocolate and assorted candies for decoration

Directions

1. Preheat oven to 400° F and grease the mini donut tray with butter.
2. Sift the dry ingredients together.
3. In a separate bowl whisk egg, melted butter, milk, and vanilla extract.
4. Pour the wet ingredients into dry ingredients.
5. Mix until well combined.

6. Pour the batter into donut molds and bake for 15 to 20 minutes.
7. Remove and set aside.
8. For cinnamon donut, roll the donuts into cinnamon and sugar mixture.
9. Decorate some donuts with melted chocolate and candies.
10. Insert the skewer into donuts and serve.

Caramel Popcorn on a Stick

Serves 12

Ingredients

½ cup sugar

1 ½ cups brown sugar

½ cup butter

1 cup water

1 cup light corn syrup

2 teaspoons vinegar

½ teaspoon salt

10 cups popped popcorn

12 candy canes, wooden skewers, or ice pop sticks.

Directions

1. Mix both sugars, water, corn syrup, vinegar, and salt in a small sauce pan.
2. Bring the mixture to boil, stirring constantly.
3. Once the mixture starts bubbling, add a drop of the mixture into ice cold water to form a ball. If a ball forms, proceed. If not, continue boiling for 1-2 minutes more.
4. Stir in butter until melted and cook for an additional 2 minutes on low heat.
5. Remove from heat and pour the caramel over popcorn in a large bowl.
6. Stir until the popcorn is entirely coated.

7. Let the popcorn cool for 2 to 3 minutes until they are cool but slightly warm enough to mold.
8. Lightly butter your hands and shape into 12 balls.
9. Insert candy cane, skewer, or Popsicle stick and serve.

Cheesecake on a Stick

Serves 8

Ingredients

16 ounces cream cheese

¼ cup cream

½ cup sugar

1 teaspoon vanilla extract

2 eggs

8 Popsicle sticks

For crumb layer
1 cup chocolate or vanilla wafer crumb

¼ cup melted butter

For coating
2 cups melted semisweet chocolate

3 tablespoons shortening

For decoration
Vanilla-flavored candy coating

Coconut flakes

Sprinkles

Directions
1. Preheat oven to 350° F.
2. Mix crumbs and butter together in a small bowl.
3. Line an 8-inch cake pan with foil. Press the crumb mixture in the bottom of pan.

4. In a large mixing bowl, beat cream cheese and sugar. Gradually add in the eggs, cream, and vanilla extract. Beat until well combined and smooth.

5. Pour the cheese mixture over crust and bake for 30 to 40 minutes., or until set

6. Remove the cheesecake from pan and let it cool.

7. Once cooled, cut evenly into triangle, place a Popsicle sticks in bottoms of cheesecake.

8. In a heat proof bowl mix together chocolate and shortening, and microwave for about 30 seconds, until completely melted. Whisk and let it cool for 2-3 minutes.

9. Dip the cheesecake sticks in the melted chocolate, letting excess drip off.

10. Decorate with your favorite topping.

11. Freeze for 30-40 minutes and serve.

Cupcake on a Stick

Serves 15

Ingredients

1 ½ cups all-purpose flour

1 cup sugar

⅔ cup of buttermilk

6 tablespoons canola oil

2 eggs

1 ½ teaspoons baking powder

¼ teaspoon baking soda

1 teaspoon vanilla extract

¼ teaspoon salt

15 lollipop sticks

For decoration:
Some pink, yellow, and purple candy melts

1 cup melted semisweet chocolate

Glazed cherries or red candy

Sprinkles for garnishing

Directions

1. Preheat the oven to 350° F. Line mini muffin cups with paper liners.
2. In a large bowl, sift together flour, baking powder, baking soda, and salt.
3. In another bowl beat oil, sugar, vanilla extract, and eggs until it forms a creamy and frothy mixture.
4. Slowly add flour mixture to the egg mixture and mix.
5. Add in butter milk and mix it again, until smooth and well combined.
6. Fill each muffin cup ⅔ full with batter.
7. Bake for 14-16 minutes until a toothpick inserted into the center of cupcakes comes out clean.
8. Let cool completely on a wire rack.
9. Line a baking sheet with parchment paper; set aside.
10. Dip each bottom of the cupcakes into melted chocolate and place it on the prepared baking sheet. Refrigerate until chocolate is set.
11. Melt candy melts into separate bowls.
12. Dip each cupcake top into the candy melts.
13. Top with a glazed cherry and some sprinkles and refrigerate until candy melt is set.
14. To serve , insert lollipop sticks into bottom of each cupcake Serve and enjoy.

Chocolate Kiwi Pops

Serves 8

Ingredients

4 kiwis

1 cup semi-sweet chocolate chunks or chips

1 teaspoon coconut oil or butter

Rainbow sprinkles to decorate (optional)

8 Popsicle sticks

Directions

1. Peel and cut the ½ inch thick slices of kiwi.
2. Melt the chocolate and oil together in a microwave safe bowl.
3. Insert Popsicle sticks into each kiwi slice and dip them into melted chocolate. Use sprinkles to decorate the pops.
4. Place them onto a baking sheet lined with wax paper.
5. Refrigerate for 30 minutes or until chocolate has fully set.

Peach Pie on a Stick

Serves 24

Ingredients

1 package refrigerated pie crust

1 cup canned peach pie filling

1 large egg yolk

24 lollipop sticks

Directions

1. Preheat oven to 375° F. Line two cookie sheets with parchment paper.
2. On a lightly floured surface, roll the dough out, about ¼ inch thick rectangle. Using a round cookie cutter or a small glass, cut out circles.
3. Spoon a small amount of peach pie filling into the centers of each half of cutouts.
4. Brush with the egg yolk around the perimeter of the circles and press lollipop sticks gently into the pastry cutouts, about 2/3 way deep.
5. Top with the second pastry cutout and seal the edges with a fork.
6. Brush the pie pops with egg yolk.
7. Bake until crust is nice golden brown, about 15 minutes.

Strawberry Shortcake on a Stick

Serves 12

Ingredients

1 package frozen biscuit dough

1 cup heavy cream

1 teaspoon vanilla extract

12 strawberry

2 tablespoons sugar

12 wooden skewers

Directions

1. Cut the biscuit dough into 1 inch thick cubes and bake according to the package directions.
2. Let cool.
3. Slice the strawberries into halves.
4. In a small bowl whip cream, sugar, and vanilla extract and transfer it to a piping bag.
5. Now thread a chunk of biscuit, then whipped cream and then sliced strawberry onto skewer.
6. Serve chilled.

S'mores Pops

Serves 20

Ingredients

1 ½ cups semi-sweet chocolate chips

10 graham crackers

20 marshmallows

20 lollipop sticks

Directions

1. In a food processor, pulse graham cracker until crumbs are formed. Place the crumbs onto a plate.
2. Now thread the marshmallow onto the lollipop sticks.
3. Melt the chocolate chips in a large bowl.
4. Working quickly, dip the marshmallow into chocolate then roll into the graham cracker crumbs.
5. Place S'more pops on a baking sheet lined with parchment paper or a large cup. Refrigerate for 30 minutes until chocolate hardens.

Apple Fritters on a Stick

Serves 15

Ingredients

3 cups all-purpose flour

4 to 5 apples, peeled, chopped into ¼ inch chunks

3 tablespoons sugar

1 ¾ cups of milk

1 egg

1 tablespoon melted butter

2 ½ teaspoons baking powder

½ teaspoon baking soda

1 teaspoon vanilla extract

1 cup confectioner's sugar or melted chocolate

1 cup peanuts, chopped

1 cup oil

15 wooden skewers

Directions

1. In a large mixing bowl mix together flour, sugar, baking powder, and baking soda.
2. In a separate bowl whisk together egg, milk, vanilla extract, and butter.
3. Now fold the dry ingredients into the wet ingredients. Mix until smooth and lump free.
4. Add the chopped apple chunks to the batter.

5. Heat the oil in a large skillet over medium heat.
6. Now drop a tablespoon of batter into the hot oil, 4 to 5 fritters at a time.
7. Fry until nice golden brown and drain on a paper towel.
8. Place the fritters into confectioner sugar or melted chocolate to coat completely.
9. Sprinkle with some chopped peanuts.
10. Insert the skewer and serve.

Banana Split Treats on a Stick

Serves 9

Ingredients

3 large bananas

12 strawberries

12 brownie, 1 inch pieces

12 fresh pineapple, 1 inch chunks

½ cup peanuts, chopped

½ cup pecans, chopped

9 Wooden skewers

Melted chocolate

Whipping cream

Directions

1. Remove the tops from strawberries. Slice the banana's into 1/2 inch thick.
2. Now place one sliced banana, one pineapple, one strawberry, and a piece of brownie onto each skewer.
3. Drizzle each skewer with some melted chocolate and sprinkle with chopped peanuts and pecans.
4. Serve with whipped cream and melted chocolate.

Fruity Ice Pops

Serves 12

Ingredients

3 cups orange juice

1 cup fresh strawberries

1 cup fresh blueberries

1 cup kiwi, peeled and diced

1 peach, peeled, cored, and diced

12 ice pop molds or small plastic cups

12 ice pop sticks

Directions

1. Place the mixed fruits into a bowl and stir to mic. Divide fruits evenly between ice pop molds.
2. Pour the juice into the molds, insert Popsicle sticks and freeze for 6 hours or overnight.

Chocolate Bacon on a Stick

Serves 15

Ingredients

1 pound bacon, thick sliced

1 cup semi-sweet chocolate chips

5 tablespoons heavy cream

½ cup maple syrup

15 wooden skewers

For topping:
Crystallized ginger

Caramelized almonds

Roasted coconut flakes

Directions

1. Preheat the oven to 400° F.
2. Thread each bacon strip weaving back and forth onto skewers.
3. Place on a large baking sheet, lined with parchment paper.
4. Drizzle maple syrup on both the sides of skewer.
5. Bake for 25 minutes or until bacon is crisp.
6. Drain on paper towels, and allow to cool completely at room temperature.
7. Add the chocolate chips in a small bowl and melt in the microwave. Let cool down a few minutes before adding the cream. Whisk the cream and chocolate together until smooth.

8. Let stand for 3-4 minutes until set.
9. Drizzle chocolate sauce over each bacon.
10. Sprinkle with your favorite toppings and refrigerate until chocolate is set.

Pineapple Funnel Cake

Serves 12

Ingredients

2 cups all-purpose flour

1 ½ cups pineapple, 1 inch chunks

2 tablespoons sugar

1 ½ cups milk

1 teaspoon pineapple extract

2 eggs

1 teaspoon baking powder

½ teaspoon cinnamon

¼ teaspoon salt

½ cup of confectioner's sugar

<u>For drizzling:</u>
Melted chocolate

Strawberry syrup

Oil for frying

12 wooden skewers

Directions

1. In heavy skillet, heat oil at 375° F.
2. In a large bowl combine flour, sugar, baking powder, cinnamon, and salt.
3. In a separate bowl whisk eggs, pineapple extract, and milk together.

4. Pour the egg mixture into the dry ingredients and mix until smooth.
5. Carefully fold in the pineapple chunks.
6. Spoon a small amount of batter into oil and fry until golden brown.
7. Remove and drain on paper towel.
8. Roll the balls into confectioner's sugar.
9. Insert wooden skewer and serve warm.

Rainbow Lollipop

Serves 4

Ingredients

2 ¾ cups sugar

¼ cup corn syrup

⅛ teaspoon cream of tartar

¾ cup water

2 teaspoons lemon juice

¼ teaspoon strawberry extract

¼ teaspoon pineapple extract

¼ teaspoon mint extract

3 gel food coloring, preferably red, yellow, and green.

4 lollipop sticks

Small plastic treat bags

10 yards curling ribbon (optional)

Cotton gloves covered in silicone gloves to manipulate the hot candy

Directions

1. Preheat oven to 300° F. Line a baking sheet with baking paper.
2. In a large sauce pan over medium heat, mix together sugar, corn syrup, and water. Bring to boil. Once boiling, insert a candy thermometer and let it boil, until it reaches to 295° F.

3. Once it reaches 295° F, remove it from heat and stir in cream of tartar and lemon juice. Allow it to sit until it stops bubbling, about 8 to 10 minutes.
4. Transfer the candy mixture into 4 different bowls, stir in strawberry extract with red food coloring in one bowl, pineapple extract and yellow coloring into the second, mint extract and green food coloring into the third one, and leave the last bowl simply white.
5. Place the baking sheet in oven for 30 seconds to warm up.
6. Transfer the red candy mixture onto the warm baking sheet for 30 seconds.
7. Stretch the warm candy mixture until it becomes opaque and shiny.
8. Repeat the same technique with rest of the candy mixture, one color at a time.
9. Warm up them all candies slightly on a baking sheet for 15 seconds.
10. Mix together all four of the candy mixtures to make a thick cylinder.
11. Evenly divide the cylinder into 4 pieces, and roll them out into thin strips.
12. Insert a lollipop stick into the one end of strip and roll inward, going round and round to make lollipop.
13. Don't over roll to make a giant lollipop; sticks might not hold the weight. Keep them small.
14. Place each lollipop into a plastic treat bag and tie bag with a bow, if desired, made with the ribbon.

Hot Chocolate on a Stick

Serves 25

Ingredients

18 ounces chopped semi-sweet chocolate or chips

4 ounces chopped unsweetened chocolate or chips

½ cup heavy cream

14 ounces sweetened condensed milk

Dozens candy cane pieces or mini marshmallows for decoration

Nonstick cooking spray

Milk to serve

25 lollipop sticks

Directions

1. Grease the mini muffin cups or ice cube tray with nonstick cooking spray.
2. Place the chopped semi-sweet and unsweetened chocolate in a large heat proof bowl.
3. In a small sauce pan whisk together cream and condensed milk, on medium heat whisking continuously bring the mixture to boil.
4. Once the mixture simmers, immediately pour the cream over chopped chocolate pieces and let it set for a minute.
5. Whisk the cream and chocolate until it forms a thick, shiny, and smooth mixture.
6. Pour the chocolate into the prepared molds.

7. Allow the mixture to set completely by tapping the mold onto the counter a few times. Even out the top with a flat spatula or knife.

8. Insert lollipop sticks and decorate with your favorite toppings.

9. Refrigerate for overnight.

10. Serve with a glass of warm milk.

Pina Colada on a Stick

Serves 12

Ingredients

20-25 pineapple, 1 inch chunks

7 ounces white rum

6 ounces coconut cream

1 tablespoon fresh lime juice

12 wooden skewer or bamboo sticks

Directions

1. Preheat grill to high.
2. In a small bowl whisk together coconut cream, rum, and lime juice. Set aside.
3. Thread 4 to 5 chunks of pineapple onto skewer.
4. Grill the pineapple skewers on each side until grill marks appear.
5. Serve with coconut cream dip.

About the Author

Louise Davidson is an avid cook who likes simple flavors and easy-to-make meals. She lives in Tennessee with her husband, her three grown children, her two dogs, and the family's cat, Whiskers. She loves the outdoor and has mastered the art of camp cooking on open fires and barbecue grills.

In colder months, she loves to whip up some slow cooker meals, and uses her favorite cooking tools in her kitchen, the cast iron pans, and Dutch oven. She also is very busy preparing Christmas treats for her extended family and friends. She gets busy baking for the holiday season sometimes as early as October. Her recipes are cherished by everyone who has tasted her foods and holiday treats.

Louise is a part-time writer of cookbooks, sharing her love of food, her experience, and her family's secret recipes with her readers.

She also loves to learn and share tips and tricks to make life a breeze.

More Books by Louise Davidson

Here are some of Louise Davidson's other cookbooks. You can click on the covers to take a look at any of them.

You can also visit her author's page here:

https://www.amazon.com/Louise-Davidson/e/B00MD2U4S6/ref=dp_byline_cont_pop_ebooks_1

Appendix – Cooking Conversion Charts

1. Measuring Equivalent Chart

Type	Imperial	Imperial	Metric
Weight	1 dry ounce		28g
	1 pound	16 dry ounces	0.45 kg
Volume	1 teaspoon		5 ml
	1 dessert spoon	2 teaspoons	10 ml
	1 tablespoon	3 teaspoons	15 ml
	1 Australian tablespoon	4 teaspoons	20 ml
	1 fluid ounce	2 tablespoons	30 ml
	1 cup	16 tablespoons	240 ml
	1 cup	8 fluid ounces	240 ml
	1 pint	2 cups	470 ml
	1 quart	2 pints	0.95 l
	1 gallon	4 quarts	3.8 l
Length	1 inch		2.54 cm

* Numbers are rounded to the closest equivalent

2. Oven Temperature Equivalent Chart

T(°F)	T(°C)
220	100
225	110
250	120
275	140
300	150
325	160
350	180
375	190
400	200
425	220
450	230
475	250
500	260

* $T(°C) = [T(°F)-32] * 5/9$
** $T(°F) = T(°C) * 9/5 + 32$
*** Numbers are rounded to the closest equivalent

Printed in Poland
by Amazon Fulfillment
Poland Sp. z o.o., Wrocław